D1602801

BOOKS BY JOHN COLETTI

Mum Halo (Rust Buckle Books, 2010)

Skasers with Anselm Berrigan (Flowers & Cream, 2012)

DEEP CODE

CITY LIGHTS SPOTLIGHT SERIES NO. 12

JOHN COLETTI

DEEP

CODE

CITY LIGHTS

SAN FRANCISCO

CONTENTS

CITY LIGHTS SPOTLIGHT
The City Lights Spotlight Series was founded in 2009,
and is edited by Garrett Caples.

Library of Congress Cataloging-in-Publication Data
Coletti, John.
[Poems. Selections]
Deep code / John Coletti.
pages cm. — (City lights spotlight ; 12)
ISBN 978-0-87286-649-2 (paperback)
I. Title.
PS3603.O4365A6 2014
811'.6—dc23
2014023853

Cover Image: *intooutof* (2001) [detail], graphite on paper, 37"x32" by Dean
Smith. Copyright © 2001 Dean Smith. deansmith.us

All City Lights Books are distributed to the trade by
Consortium Book Sales and Distribution: www.cbsd.com

For small press poetry titles by this author and others,
visit Small Press Distribution: www.spdbooks.com

City Lights Books are published at the City Lights Bookstore,
261 Columbus Avenue, San Francisco, CA 94133
www.citylights.com

DEEP CODE

EXPLOSIVELY RATIONAL

We keep ruining our lives to be wonderful

I am not

convinced

but

neither am I   unconvinced

the primary colors go

one, two, three

red, yellow, and blue

BROKEN LEG

One for home, for job, for debt
for squirms, for love
flap, flap, flap, page, page, page
scrutinized by a figurine Hermes
all the crazy shit I did tonight
(last night)
sleepwalking w/ a snake, red cross
Peugot lion
extra freaky
and sort of in song, ex fabris
chestnut
stuns eyes
reminds me I'm meat
gives me goose bumps
stopping to look

DUKES UP

The Easter egg hunt
inherently cruel
religiously obscene
"I see one." "Let me get one."
tears. like that.
an epiphenomenelogical account from like organisms
teasing @ the homegrown
in a banged-up locker
that convince me, at the end of darknessses
that I want to enjoy being family-kept-spilling
I never understate
& demonstrate daily
the capital shock then "wooed
& won by wireless"
weeds I thought more beautiful tilted
like a panix' serpent
calming
core doubts. it's been a little rough.
pancakes at midnight
pancakes at day

Medieval reenactors
dragging
that one aria
from Turandot
around your eye. forever closed
the tingling of clean, crystal lights
then laid back down. don't rot: sayeth Beaker
the tendered non-capital evening
a third wave: Starting fresh!

MEME

Yoda biofeedback
glass
"when wild things happen
we behave like ourselves"
Danish Crown
spit
into
mattress blower
a debauched
week
yes
it
has
been
so
high tide
glue
anti-glue
endless
fml. iaf. uul. fire

Truffaut-ian
lion mane
summer / ceiling
demon-gaze
vacation-
spiked
steak
mounting
Andrew: lulz
annoyed
by the truth venom
god damnit | OFF
trying not to get ^%#$ or @#%$&
tonight
pushups
& angry birds
Best Western
Pepto salmon egg caviar
I thought to make an import export of it
something very shady
and underground

RECOVERY

b/c it can't transcribe
our own handwriting
sneak into the Met
in back of the gift shop
ascending the staircase
Picasso lithos $4,000
Glorification
of the Giustiani
Tiepolo 1784-1785
Goya's Manuel Osorio
Manrique de Zuñiga
in bright orange-
based red
holding a pet magpie on a string
calling card
in mouth
Jan Gossaert
Antwerp
mannerism
cluttered compositions

in elegant poses
exaggerated
draperies
& excessive
embellishments
of all kinds

(DANA @ DENNY'S)

I don't want much, but I want ALLLLLLL the experience
put on Charlie Rose
eat cupcakes
HELMET SMASH
read the birth story
over iPhone
& it felt like
it was
the end
& beginning of writing
I'm going to be 23 Tuesday
51 Wednesday
Dale Jr.
shredding an axe on a cascade of sparks
"U around beauty face?"
"What else man?"
"I had a dream about us the other day
duh / I was among
the gods of Olympus
living on the Rhine, and we both rowed crew"
"Jesus Christ. bye honey
my day won't get any better."

GUILT SWEEP ·

Broke J's pipe
cooking up
Legal Defense
for some Muppets
smoking tinseltoe
under
Charles North's
choir angels
on
AQUARIUM
BRAWL
rainin' blood
& lovin it
all over
Aerosmith
& Zeppelin
in the milk canoe
being
a psychopath w/
ethics / an
Epic Mountain Cat

PARK SLOPE METAL BAR

The Jesus flowers are irises
playing kicker w/ the workers
amidst these great arches:
Metal for the Masses, Astrid Swan
Truck Fighters, Coq Eyes
Fuck the Commerce XI, With Full Force
Fire Razor, Sticky Handshake
Tie Me Up w/ Goons, Bag Full of Nickels
Feast of Bad Intentions, Designed
for Your Children To Have Just One
Donkey, Ultimate High
Dirty Pool, Day Shades
Good? Good, Das Funfen Finale
100 Times Before, The Walk of Shame
Theater 89, 20 Years, Dating Your Skeletons
the indigestible hurl
of pyramids, purple-pink

EVIDENT SOURCE

My brother, my father
my dearest friend
filth. filth. you are nothing but
filth, Stonehenge
on the 12:32 a.m. pizza
scattered, partied-out
like science on daisies
Micah in green water
though we lay broken
slowly, rolling the whip out
by Bergen & 5th
the lilt in yr heart
I can change—
all puffy-mooned
exhausted
Helvetica
Neue
trees on it, shrapnel
dancing up & down
the mall

plush-stuffed
adorable
hostile Cylon
in treatment silence
Happy Baby
fucked me up—
or so you thought
pinned to an 8-wheeler
when you reached into the empty
& came up sun
out on sad-period-wretch
well, we may never be friends. but
I went upstairs to chip @ some floor oats
pill-popping
a fridge's
shameless selfies
lint-up . . . beasts . . .
I mean
use fears people!
o parental Control
"How way way the fuck up there"
garage-banging
waterbeds, by the permanently

accessible & emotionally dodgy

Amway representatives

I welcome

now shaving off frost

Dixie's old qualities divided of   undignified well . . .

      but still, today was a really nice day

             just wasn't you

charged,

exhausted

late-stage adult acne

        magic markers

            all over the temples

                                    borrowed trophies

                        obsolete failures

three weepy bracelets

drifting

two @ a time

       undoing the

   tenderness

of a youthful   meta-cluck

tagged-back

             by social mediocrity

being that fallow
"oh I hate them"
@ the end of purity ____

Countless   snags
saying
yes to a fab-brand   of mild cynicism

Devotional ESP
& a nail ripping through its   cargo spit-Ats   slipping offline
to devote   long-hair truckyards   to available roe:

Ear drums w/ coffee shakes
            super crispy
all outline   deities born   cutup fall
life as oil drum   nice guy's dreamcatchers   toxic face   in
behavior wash

Ouched by posters of desperation
& the most miniature talon
I will not re-reproduce
face of a fool, yes, for many I've been

PAINFUL TO WATCH

"I some-
times cry
a lot
for no reason."
eye in
white
lettering
quick cement

OF BLOOD DRIFTS, SQUEAK

(shit have a few manners)
who aggrieved. look down
unsubtle memory
mid-wave huff kelp
lost in self-annihilation
someone's agitant
of warm shame
per core / acrobatic
inconviction / the next
sugar-crunch of
kind in stuffed gold
sheepish snow parents
or rose-water crud
many captains sold-out by
winning over the pissoir's
self-juiced dome
heavy bag in heavy bag

STATE NAME

Of pleasure, to connect physically
powerfully, that I
love you w/ the power of another talking to
and will let you
touch my lips
make them stop
Bontecou
light bulb in the shape of
a grotesque water lily
awful steel
Mephistophelean lilt
loose white
muscles my ears
breathing orange irises w/ a good chest shave
vampire gatherer
Bols Campari Bols
peacock feather
earrings
apricot brandy
up the neck

in sharp eggshell
armadillo tail
wisps of untidy hair
hanging from the wall
putting on my old clothes
inner Griswold
Thurman accordion
they know the end is
meaningless because
I break free
you heard me
you heard
what I said
burnt eyelashes
through a tiger on a bike
clubbed little ends stuck together
for supreme sense of structure
the world is not his mine or ice
exposure w/ veins
I don't fit in
an adorable photograph
you keep behind
a menagerie of things

we refuse to move
tho clash and clutter
together in the corn flakes
a little grain sugar
sneaking
around broken trains
bored with the recipe
blowing superior raspberries
you never grow
just results
"poet as fuck right now"
a painting at Julia's
in low cut Grecian dress
looking into a mirror pool
the whole canvas
falling into and crashing the disturbance
the ripple *inside pleasure*
one dark red braid
of C. I dreamt last night
her eyes had that extra left them in them
an insecure penny
full of quitting streams
waving a cigar gasmask back at the Republik

puffin
Coca-Cola
every head turning
beautiful nuns
on an unwiped sooty table
flecked on mirror globe
peeling potatoes in Delfian light
her bonnet the benefit of
surviving Twix
frozen rolls
sexualized years
the inside winter
stacked and forgotten
I'm doing exactly what I'm meant to be doing
waiting to
desperate?
give in forever
life isn't only for the final fifteen
I wonder do I stop
pressing these buttons right
here, reducing
humility into caricature
a shaggy sheepdog

encased in unrippable foil
LIDL in the permafrost
itching elbows
to reduce tension
thighs
belching to
the assembled virtues of your past empty selves
meanwhile young men die for lack
of true results
that alpha pair destroying hardened unto
weak bigotry, our nerves . . . or others
. . . their biases, impatient
not ours but wholly sanctioned by the cartoon
of our culture severely mismanaged
and perverted by the switch
on the broken crucifix of
unspeakable conscience
fed closet after closet of
misguided fashion
shivers from
a misfed ark
watching me be somebody
on top of someone else

anybody
am I going to learn
tonight to be
the proper shame
the one who counts

MR. HIGH NIPPLES

Champagne cocktails & Sade
crushed Pringles in a water glass
watching Crispy Hills
half-naked at Earl Hall
70% current body weight
throwing tantrums
w/ a sort of English purity
spit strawberry pie in a bucket
then totally unscramble
& gargle some Schweppes
Super Beast like we were
just heaving armies
of great men
hump-worthy adorable
totally click click click
your life on fire right?
bing bang popcorn

CATTYWUMPUS

Pitch-
drip
1.3 mph
slower
than
you
think
unique upper-poverty / like you had the choice
Autocannibal
MFA
d'macro—
approach
backwood-
belch-
ing
by
Johnny
Go Boom
in immense paralysis
that the drop

does
fall
a bit
slower than
u
think
damaged or getting over
Nights in Fairmont
as the sid is gred
the knee . . .
the knuckle . . .
the golden glow
asteroid-mining
bowling-ball
airplane town's unrecognizable phone number
the final
outpost's
retraumatized bridgeway
that piece of yr heart's
personal
Condiment
I'd earned
when I was

a decent person
but therapy
said: "No. No more . . ."
of that
bright
pidgeon
then came on the
tiddlywinks
well,
you don't have to
  be rich
   to be
 cuffing
each pant leg
playing dangerous bargain w/
unethical & delicate, yet
under the Xmas tree you
don't get to bully me
but: "I think you should write a poem about how we watched Paris
        '71 there
that my bike on the corner, being a great metaphor for
why everything seems so difficult
when all I want to do is

raise everyone up
not having to trust anyone or
lay myself on them in protective regret."
& as "my baggage . . .
has baggage"
If you follow,
I'll follow
the miracle lint bent of its bulb
well
I guess
Shaggies won—
the lifestyle non-fight
of pre-hot-
daube
teaching
heathens | Genesis
part figure | part light
an Orleans
of self re-recovery
cut-off-in-
auxiliary:
so I What To
Wear this?

hat
all the time?
OK
so now, what?
reaction time
+
assumptions
+
oops, you wrong
      Crib toad:
    Gremlin / PAUSE
preacher   fuzz
according to Southern Rules of Hunting:
for this title: "Unserveable"
I know . . .
I know . . .
Children are awful
they stare
too much
@ bold abstraction
Thanks Shane
thank you so much
for thanking me . . .

so taste of the delicacies
red panda
statue   outside
Holy Cow   I *do not* like
how plain   yr tenderness is

I AM NOT MYSELF

I'm severely everyone
& it hurts

if I'm sick
you'll take care of me?

"Oh, yeah
sure
of course."

COUNTRY STRONG

Civically challenged
three raptors
one on each other's back
shoveling snow
into the Great White roll
no longer a primate in crisis
To sea. To sea.
must be Friday.
Craig Carton
Curtis Sliwa
Major World
KFC
Bucket List Chart of
Extreme Ambivalence
1921: Duchamp
U.S. Open's for you
in slight rain hieratic
emerald white
soft sunset pooka shells
broadcast sports   being unemployed's

kind of like
Sunday morning
every day
grasping, sighing, overthinking.

GASOLINE: TOYS

2011. The Roman tomb of
Shelley
no longer in fashion
like unto choir bullies infected by
Bergson in a hissy
the best of the
Gowanus
belched
What's happening
is this Candyland? Let go.
Let go of the cardboard Op
minty fresh Oops.
or was it Big Beep?
your life's work
in an uninterested hour
put down the chili
the semi-goop
"But what is he saying? Who cares?! It is said!
'Outside by a Halloween fire,
wise on a charred log,

an old man dictating to the heir of the Goon.'"
There's golfing yet
glove yr hand
in obscene
pillow
beside couch
not in it
grand Cru
olton Wanderers
playing harp for B
in a fight for sixth place
on the list of Best Facial Cleansers
see them close. 2008
boat
feeding
tiger eye
Cambridge
Colossus
smoked
into cuppy hands
must watch
lips
pouring bubbly

into beagle's mouth
iPhone
to iPhone
duck mouth
gone dirty
tilted
down
Rollie Fingers
up
the X Facture
spirit's
manufactured   excitement
Aeolian harp
unwashed inside
wetting cloth
lime, laubling blau
Menale's cross
Suarez
Monster Drink
mixed by
Silver
Spoon
doing a séance
with Corso

tossed over the city
his teeth taste like Equal
Zuul
Wait . . . am I
still? chores
doing shores
on the low
da'usa
(yoouish.) . . .
Hodiernis Europeis
this shadow be legion
300 prickly
thorns
mailing me
Botox-approved
incisors
airlines
incontinence
might go to bed, but
the floor lacked
such shards
I thought
adorable
watered-down

half-sleeping
sea-
beasty
confectioner's
might
doom?
Definitely.
Probably?
Nah.
the headphones?
waited
gremlins?
me: RUN
!
Dustin:
YES!
celebrate
light switch. it's
been real fun-
disgusting
mice
w/koans
I'm
their

problem
now
ball eroded by
plaster Georgian horse
& a nasty
resin
thread
click
meaningless
sucking
sure
the magnets
lack morals
tipped by
a wheedwhacker
sorry
are you?
nodules
declined by abject
beat
normal hurt?
the fern of an elk
was that all

YESTERDAY'S PAPERS

I touch gentle people

in peaceful ways

albeit

aggressively

at the heart

only one way

to love

don't

break easily

ST. JEROME

@ the Doria
Pamphilj
4,745 calories
over-budget
playing ping-
pong
in rain
kind of crushed
may not make it
well
all the
clocks say
different things
GI Joe in the daisies
cleaned up by
shaky blood
& the hustle

BEAT INSIDE

Walking the world w/ a pot scarf
a placard, a fist, and a pension
working the system
all that money spent on grass
lip-twitching for days
effortlessly
preening best qualities
You can tell Jo. Half-Baked
got me through it. then
got tremendously sad
& remembered
what it felt like to be consumed and lonely
wept for Swank. felt meek
winning the series   by myself
will fall. will all. and skewer
each of my marriages: each
supports me
just recently—things I've heard.

THE RECITATION OF THE PROBLEM

AFTER PAUL THEK

"Goodbye,
bye water"

then tilts
and

falls backwards

pushing around empty strollers:

when I let go

typo
baggies
mmm. yes, yum.

bad possum.
OK sure I'll do

oops don't
print that

not so much   hug love?

got plenty

skip cats

be beautified

Christian smalljoy
big courage FAIL

won't answer

gauzy Bruce
Getty damn.   ask.
        like

community
            attentivey

serious

spiritual hernia

I'LL SHOW YOU

On my way to M's
I develop a fever
gone all summer
very Ara Oacus
and in the end isn't
that why I go
into the evitable
never remains
devotional ablutions
crash earlier, wake earlier
passing Rome's
French Academy
more interested
in my ways
than my means
accept that critics
reek reek terribly
wiped ink
remembered for
an introductory note

I love being
committed
to frivolous things
all the way
fully clothed
like sipped from
the cloudiness
don't fear massive staircase
the old cartoon drinking songs
where parents act like
they don't want it
knee deep in "pucker slop"
doing makeup in Hartford
fritillary teasles
blown onto cut-up
Pop Rocks
One Anthem
"with a slow curve"
gone to scratch
the resistible
day glow sandwich wrap
spitting on
the wrong career

"I celebrate our openness."
is a cute thing to say
"Are you still a dick?"
"I am." "He likes me?"
"I'm sure." the deep
assholishness
of this guy
gives me writer's block
& a pleasant white marsh
busy understanding
obliviousness w/
a high end sports car
covered in
Superman plastic
Connecticut flags
wasted on Hart Street
a lifelong beating
in mills, ships, and factories
the cigarette freedom of
debt free living
optics / emotions / confusions
art's deeply feeling lost

COMPARATIVE PAIN

FOR CHARLES

Father's Day at the Turkey's Nest
defeated by Tapper
home by whennish
beat up and sub-optimal
a fried U
sleeping peacefully
mermaid
Jawa
Major
Backpack
Party Boats
cut off
to kick out
the misery
East coast skaters
just failed brats
on ecstasy
& I could be one of them

if I weren't so heavy
my name? "I do"
and do it brilliantly

POST-IT

Dear cage—would I
really question
love? immediate, true,
& incredibly false
"paid to play
w/ broken toys"
only love
can't overcome
the beast, Brittle
as I am
clapping hands
your chin
bundled in mine

COUCH COMFORT THEORY

Maradona jumping into his assistant's belly
to media
in tights
all of the child in him
down the frame
of my bike
losing touch w/
where Lebron
might be turning
sleeping on an Aerobed
in our old place
buy a book
on immediate Buddhism
fear humility
fear humility less
then all went pear-shaped
" / . . . . . / "
cummerbunds
rosemary
leaves

"I may."
"Maw may."
"Mom. Me."
made a teenager
who will
make me money
playing hide and seek
w/ the fares
kindly tolerated
one eye
bloodshot
gathering
wood
Dave Hickey thinks
we wouldn't need love songs if we weren't
hot sex & baby making
maybe
I got that all backwards?
make many love songs
but that's. well
you know
270/12
broadly cast in forever

lined up for a sack race
to cool your toes
a towel
around
each
lawn
sprinkler
zombie
state
public
hoof

PINK & GRAY SWATCH

Strawberry Shortcake
Care Bear diary
padlock open
furry and rubbable
Journey on
bangs cut
@ brow point
individual servings of
grit, we live on
it; we're cheap.
naked from the buckles up

AND MARKS ME ON THE KNUCKLE
WITH A BLUE MARK

Faded-St. Louis tie
matching J'VON
Crew Member
w/ CHRISTA
Crew Member
Trader Joe's badges
Santa stocking
transformer bazooka
bike lock, Reaperbot
key, diagram of heart
2 angles (medical)
buckets, unchecked
triceratops & the bad glue
that made us good friends
watching winter's mirage twist
out-parting nervousness
"Why won't you
just take me

to Olive Garden?"
too busy (pumping shoulders)
ain't seen those eyes in a while

SHRIGLEY

Eagle Tanker   time to shreeeeeed

lost the light?

all light.

all light.

ARCHERY?

Fuck them!   & their arrows!
their arrows
and their bows . . .
their chimes & their arrows
Big beers. Big beers for Brad.
1-800-LAWYER
But also.
Who cares?
"This is the reason
bald men
like tailoring"
then what?   then nothing

MONTSERRAT

"Crisis" fold clothes
feel the diodes
such a lovely voice
ah, & etc. gibberish
draped in by Marcel
Broodthaers
where'd my friends go?
"We quit." "Oh, thank god."
You've been learned.
"It's real art not Picasso."
Jean Dior slammed
at Bonita II
fluff-cluttered
as we whollop w/ beach balls:
Mendelssohn
in profile
El Greco in rain
you sense it; I can't
see them yes, he's
very controlling

yr tray of Cokes:
perhaps I'm not
Shaky Nerves II
swim sandals
at the Gershwin
night-dreaming lyrics
inflammable thread
so I said the same thing
to a snail in the pool
Scottsdale's not so bad
but Phoenix is O well-
wilted lettuce you bike snob
you cow come true
give into the Brodey wig
now do it w/ me

THE SEMPER AUGUSTUS

Though I nod off now
for natural reasons
stagger in let her fall
half-asleep
removing my own hardware
the great sonnets were arbitrary
forms kept in place
by available species
Swan Lake is hard
feed your brain
when it hurts
I have an awful gift
it's telling you stop

NORTHERN NEW YORK

I spin around
my little heart
for which
I care not
smell of cow
smoked beer
strong cheese
Schenectady
grizzly
fur, two hawks
chasing a golden eagle
around
Danziger
Straße
south of Bayreuth
on a bus
w/o a toilet
that sleep is, after all
a faith

farmland
nest
cable knit sweaters

OH GOD, WAIT

Gel-haired American Apparel lump
nut down gumdrop
syllable breakdown
oh lobe lobe lobe splash splash purge
Kodiak haute bug Gump tooth dip
boned up on MASH
clutching Purell Ambesol
Bergen etiquette's all night lolli
tender O grudgingly
almost faded
Ten High Kentucky
dropping trow
some lazy mind crisp on the B60 bus
rehab w/ nameplate
near LOVE GOATS in Sharpie
I'm Danny Hoagie
and I need a whole floor
psychological folk
tinkling on top of the needy

wet Brillos menaced by union of
Central and Shed
I'm nearly home is what everyone says

'TIT REX

Late Scorpions Bishop   Splat
totally re-traumatized
by Dan Smith watching Fire Walk with Me
on the bed
w/ a big bag of Buffalo Kettle Chips
"and scene"
there is no privacy
except   in publicity
Thompson's Water Seal
as a marble   in tragic disgust
LDS   Shit Robot
                  Soft Power
plus Normal
Disaster
pre-psychotics   distressed by abstract pain
Trans-Am 2006 packing in Low-cal Gatorade®
all that teenage math traitor non-normative marine in me
a pop star, woe
like eggs—young, enormous
say yerp

says kaysies
a phone
that pulled out   pulled back in

COMPLIMENTARIES

Bifocals & rowdy geese
the whole wardrobe
of thorns & light
cut down, rearranged
our godly
plantlings. I'd
found a rock
a single rock.
Trouncing kudzu
w/ a baton
mostly given up
& settled
Jesus COPS
is depressing
the well pays out
its chronicle
of blunders
LIFE COACH
brought to you by

our good friends @ Weave
most radical
dependant, independent . . .

ELEGANT SCRIPT

Three pink slips
& eyes to match
I'm inelegant.
I prize that.
Directive please. Make rent.

POST & UNEVEN

FOR ALLI WARREN

Monster in the Pythic sense
ever-present, yet
ne'er destroyed nor
shrunken man-ram, nay
bigger proportion
Mirror salutes mirror
on Administrative
Services
Appreciation Day
"I want to do swords"
& feel as passionate
about companies
green w/ envy
as I do, against this grieve
or "afford this shit
six-legged cow"
"It's not J.D. cool,
but it's cool"

at the Big Table
familiarizing oneself
with the enemy
or narrative environments
where the only phrase
I could / write
for an hour was
"say something sweet to me"
the only phrase I could write
for an hour
sofa-umping for the obscene
Mogwai's
Ethical Delicacy
smelling of
small oranges   in a pretty   green bottle

                                        PCP
                            gone

                                            Anti-Clown
            or . . .   emotional flexibility

                        paw
                                bone
                paw
                        bone

                paw
                        bone

                        meat

        a mail-in wristwatch

    and one that looks like this:

                            bro!   brah!

    things collide, things collide on them

ON THE PAUSE

O
courage
pinhole
Captain
Co.co.

TIME TO win
really?
you 20 now?

what if I don't   wake up from the Recovery?

                              BE HELD   or

Randy   gone Friar Tuck hauling off at a Nibbler

beefing up on
Home Pride

cheese-filled

Mayer
wienies

so, spectrum

            so, tenderness

                                   so, all neurons

                   printing

                                    right

               so, tedium
so, apathy

            so, compulsory

              pegged
              capris
warm side
of the   pillow   many
eminent   lights

TOOTH TO RAILING

There exists more trouble in one day than ten make one ten I cannot
digital naïfs
throttled by Tonka Truck
Pacific ballast sharing electronic cigarettes;
this one's sweeter, less minty, a Camel
Burning Nostrils . . .
bent dimes   depressed
7 of 100
8 of 3
20 of 12
so I held up both arms in goal posts
dimmd into
the blurry shape of Decembrists
"x?"
the Artaud of enthusiasm
oven grease
sunbathing
pinwheel cubes of
long
black guava

recollection
shard's
third Croque Monsieur
antithetical to
the ethos of stupid effing
droopal tree . . .
I am the mark of
the carnally disgusting
ratty hair . . .
bleach
off bike underwater.
Plee-ay.

NATE LEMONT

The old cabbage patch goatee
w/ its stale 1980s
Blow
Pop
adhesive
yr thighbones touch my thighbones
then I put on
Body Shop
Huile de Parfum
coconut
foam finger
an editor's touch

I GUESS

my "night
out"
ended like
"this":

impeccable beauty
and the
ensuing
slug in the gut

simple forms
obtaining
Post-
Foucaultian
frigid hum

that needs
be akimbo

grown up wrong

BUT, STILL

AFTER JAY REATARD

the popcorn in the sea

no longer matters

not yet

but damn, almost I

think

of so many

damned

things

LISTENING TO THE GRAMOPHONE

In my Liz Claiborne
houndstoothe high-
shouldered
blazer from Ross
(iPhone) / wets finger
achieves retail
all that endless enthusiasm
lake after internal expression. deselect
each time the bud opens a little less

POEM

I see yr hair
coming up
Avenue of
the Americas
and it's never
been yr hair
not quite
I've been
writing in
ink again
resurrecting
the Kennedys
our daughter's
chimes
all shades
of pink
tarnished
UNC ram
sitting on
top of the

Companion
to English
Literature

SEALING TAPE BUNDLES

Walk around Venice all day
Google Earth. Pretty satisfying.
this street that one
each place I know knew
time travel exists
in yr mind w/ a crutch
puked up hipster?
last bit of goodness?
G's on shuttle
crying invisible soup
human breath
capsized
btw LP & Crescent
worth it? always
every time
leaning tower of
Smartwater
pretty you you there
all pretty
puredust & sauce splatters

.

Erasure's
incomplete
harmony
stuffed into batting cages
look pretty with apple
most beautified sweat &
fog exhaling depth
lately?
was it fucking me down?
(totally)
it was.
wasn't it?
everyone noticed

OHIO & AFTER

In the form of
decomposing
bisque—just
put ugly where ugly
already is
"icy cold"
the trumpet's lathe
"I've never slept @
yr place w/o you."
& that place
loves you
w/ great courage

DEEP CODE

Panya in cuffs
tuned up
f-inch
banana jack
phone Wrangler
palm blood
slot-car
fingertip
Rhino
Little Shits
to Horrified Man
(I can only cry at the movies
or work)
restaurant
aerosol
lepidolite
periwinkle
chalked up
ship
present

thick
thawing
chemical frost
getting laid
the cold it takes away
adjusting to a loose, black sweater
framed by
gravel, unnatural warmth
hollowed muscles
soft lips
your neck, a bicep
& tremors
playing air piano
for a map of South America
105   90   75
60   45   30
that exquisite
porcelain pen knife
w/ a painted donkey on the end
raising up from the pack
I saw a picture of Schumann the other day
& remembered
my hair clippings

paw bone
paw bone
paw bone
paw bone
how graphite shines
when you color on
color rattled like a paper match
black white black
velvet squares
abstracted
geometrically
Kermit Pez
Barney Pez
glowing
in lap
life can be tolerable
if this is the best and worst of it
yr bruised
infant cheek
frozen hands
shady eyeliner
Bosman's
wrinkled green

loam
unclean nostrils
playing
at a game of
underground dust
subtle, poor
& masochistic
a knee with a mane
trampling
over
the jelly roll quilt
everyone looks away
I thought today
that a week's stay
in a mental unit
might be a relief
god help us all
chew local
slipper
what? this is it?
just to be
at ease
w/ not being at ease

a looseness w/ punch holes
as you count
lines in flour
or the semiotics of
likelihood
in a world of
unnatural
privellage
but he was here
and I was there
to keep you
whether you would be kept or not

GET UP. YOU ALWAYS DO.

We are the Adventurers
& we are looking for a dog
but we are not the sky
looking for our heads
to be just one stare
I made you a picture of a bird
penciled in tanagers
pigeons at sea
then one much smaller I call
folded lakes
Andy Rooney's nephew
topless on a
Coney Island bench
licking 10oz road erasers
in Coke bottle glasses
just be ok for me tonight
East River's strung out headlights
still pushing through
covered buttons
I came to shoot hippos

but the digital world
barfed & won a bit
candy is delicious
you should eat some every day

The state of the world calls out for poetry
to save it. LAWRENCE FERLINGHETTI

CITY LIGHTS SPOTLIGHT SHINES A LIGHT ON THE WEALTH
OF INNOVATIVE AMERICAN POETRY BEING WRITTEN TODAY.
WE PUBLISH ACCOMPLISHED FIGURES KNOWN IN THE
POETRY COMMUNITY AS WELL AS YOUNG EMERGING POETS,
USING THE CULTURAL VISIBILITY OF CITY LIGHTS TO BRING
THEIR WORK TO A WIDER AUDIENCE. IN DOING SO, WE ALSO
HOPE TO DRAW ATTENTION TO THOSE SMALL PRESSES
PUBLISHING SUCH AUTHORS. WITH CITY LIGHTS SPOTLIGHT,
WE WILL MAINTAIN OUR STANDARD OF INNOVATION AND
INCLUSIVENESS BY PUBLISHING HIGHLY ORIGINAL POETRY
FROM ACROSS THE CULTURAL SPECTRUM, REFLECTING
OUR LONGSTANDING COMMITMENT TO THIS MOST
ANCIENT AND STUBBORNLY ENDURING FORM OF ART.

CITY LIGHTS SPOTLIGHT

1

Norma Cole, *Where Shadows Will:*
Selected Poems 1988-2008

2

Anselm Berrigan, *Free Cell*

3

Andrew Joron, *Trance Archive:*
New and Selected Poems

4

Cedar Sigo, *Stranger in Town*

5

Will Alexander, *Compression & Purity*

6

Micah Ballard, *Waifs and Strays*